THE AWARDS

THE ASSOCIATION OF PHOTOGRAPHERS THIRTEENTH AWARDS 1996

ACKNOWLEDGEMENTS

We would like to thank the following who have helped us with their time, effort and support, as well as the members of The Association of Photographers whose enthusiasm makes The Awards possible.

The Judges:
ROSIE ARNOLD
PAUL BIDDLE
DAVE BUONAGUIDI
PAUL CARBERRY
CHRIS CHEETHAM
GILL DAVIES
GARY HOLT
KIKI KENDRICK
PETER MARLOW
CAROLINE METCALFE
PETER ROBINSON
CHARLES SETTRINGTON
GEOFF SMITH
MALCOLM VENVILLE
PAUL WEBSTER

The Organisers:
SUE ALLATT
JACKIE KELLEY
VALERIE MAY
JAY MYRDAL
ANDREW OLNEY
ALEX STEELE-MORTIMER

Also:
ANNA BAILEY
DESMOND BURDON
BERNI VENT AT ALCHEMY CREATIVE SERVICES

Design, Typesetting and Artwork:
SAWARD ROBERTS
Telephone: 0171 336 7480

Front Cover Photograph:
GILES REVELL

The Association of Photographers
9-10 Domingo Street
London EC1Y 0TA
England
Telephone: 0171-608 1441 Fax: 0171-253 3007
E-Mail: aop@dircon.co.uk

Published by Reed Information Services
Windsor Court
East Grinstead House
East Grinstead
West Sussex RH19 1XA
England
Telephone: 01342 326972

Printed and Bound in Hong Kong
Produced by Mandarin Offset Limited

ISBN 0 611 00915 3

As usual, the variety and spontaneity of the photographs included has prompted much debate, as we glanced through those selected for this prestigious Awards Book.

Once again this year the selection of images shown has underlined the inspiration, vision and innate creativity which ensures that British photographers remain among the best in the world.

Whilst I am sure that all of us will have our own opinions as to the merit or otherwise of each image, what is readily apparent is the continuing quality and emerging talent of the photographers.

Congratulations from all of us at The Creative Handbook to those involved in another memorable Awards.

RICHARD WOOLLEY
Publisher

PUBLISHED BY THE MEDIA DIVISION OF REED INFORMATION SERVICES

A member of the Reed Elsevier Plc Group

If you are unable to contact any of these photographers on the telephone numbers listed, please call The Association of Photographers on 0171-608 1441

Michael Harding, Chairman, The Association of Photographers
surrounded by the Assistants who helped with the Awards judging

Photograph by Desmond Burdon
Retouching by Berni Vent at Alchemy Creative Services

It is with great pleasure that I welcome you to another collection of superb photography by Association members, both famous and less so, the greats and the soon to be greats.

Although there will always be those who imagine omissions and perceive idiosyncrasies with any awards competition such as this, I feel it more important to note our collective progression over the thirteen years of The Awards. I believe that you will find within these pages ample evidence of the steady growth in self-expression within commercial photography and the advertising, design and editorial fields we mainly work.

It must be sadly observed, however, that there continues to be pressure on photographers' rights by short-sighted elements within our potential commissioners. Our common struggle for respect and equitable treatment carries on, with The Association leading the campaign in this area, where photographers can feel isolated, vulnerable and at risk. The Association can only lead this fight. For the battle to be won, we must all realise that the self-expression we value so highly begins with self-respect; and this self-respect must mean that photographers also take steps individually to protect their own rights.

I sincerely hope that you will find creative inspiration within these pages. Furthermore, I hope that this inspiration brings renewal to those of you who find that, at times, your creative muse is battered by the ebb and flow of the daily tide of a complex modern life.

MICHAEL HARDING
Chairman, Association of Photographers

The Awards Committee: From top left

Sue Allatt, Jackie Kelley, Valerie May, Jay Myrdal, Andrew Olney, Alex Steele-Mortimer

Photograph by Desmond Burdon

Retouching by Berni Vent at Alchemy Creative Services

The Awards continue to grow year by year and while this is very good and something the Association should be proud of, this year we came dangerously close to critical mass, as far as the judging is concerned. With two thousand eight hundred photographs to view, the judging team is approaching the limit of what is physically possible. To make things even more difficult, the overall quality of the entry was, by all account, the best yet.

If the entry next year increases by the current average of 16% we will, quite frankly, be unable to process the judging in the same way. The computer system is not at fault and can cope with a considerable further increase. The problem is that it isn't really reasonable to ask a team of people to select the best 200 photographs from such a large entry of high calibre work. Many, many excellent photographs did not make it into this book for reasons which owe more to numbers than quality. In one way this is very good, and illustrates how far The Association has come over the years in its efforts to encourage the very best from our membership, but in another way we are in danger of missing the very best because the jury may no longer have the time to look at the pictures properly.

What it means is that the Association and in particular the Awards Committee and staff are going to have to examine the judging procedure again, and, I fear, make some changes for next year, to try to prevent the "lock out" that can happen to the judges when overwhelmed by a large surfeit of high quality material.

At the time of writing it is too early to say what changes will be made, but members preparing for next year's Awards should not discount further changes to the category structure, entry limits and judging procedures.

Finally I would like to invite members to join the Awards Committee to help us navigate our way through the difficulties and responsibilities of our current success.

JAY MYRDAL
Chairman of the Awards Committee

The Judges: From top left

Rosie Arnold, Paul Biddle, Dave Buonaguidi, Paul Carberry, Chris Cheetham, Gill Davies, Gary Holt, Kiki Kendrick,

Peter Marlow, Caroline Metcalfe, Peter Robinson, Charles Settrington, Geoff Smith, Malcolm Venville, Paul Webster

Photograph by Desmond Burdon

Retouching by Berni Vent at Alchemy Creative Services

Each year a panel of distinguished people from the photographic world are asked to judge The Awards. Each are highly acclaimed within their own field, and none of the judges may enter work into the Awards. The judging takes place over a gruelling two and a half days, starting with a preview of all of the images and culminating in the selection for the Awards Book, and the actual nominations for the Gold, Silver and Merit Awards. Awards do not have to be allocated – they are awarded only at the judges discretion.

This year an outstanding 2,800 images were entered into The Awards, resulting in 214 photographs being selected by 75 photographers. 26 awards were bestowed – 1 Gold, 8 Silvers and 17 Merits.

Every entry that is accepted into the Book and touring exhibition, is given a certificate. In addition to this Merit, Silver and Gold Awards may be granted. Merits must be worthy of a special mention, when work has shown an idea, approach or concept that necessitates a mention beyond that of being selected for the book. A Silver may be granted to work that has exceptional and memorable qualities, and shows even more originality. A Gold should only be awarded when all of the above qualities are combined to create a classic image, with uniqueness of concept and originality, making it a classic which will be viewed as such in years to come. And finally we have the 'Judges' Choice' allowing judges, should they wish, to individually select an image they have personally supported, but that did not get chosen by the panel as a whole. The Thirteenth Awards were announced at the Gala Presentation, at the Barbican, on Tuesday 20th February 1996.

ROSIE ARNOLD – Rosie Arnold graduated from Central School of Art & Design with a BA Hons Degree in Graphic Design. She joined Bartle Bogle Hegarty in 1983 and has worked on a wide variety of the agency's accounts, including Levi's, Pretty Polly, Puma, Radio Rentals, Liberty, The Independent and Shell. Her awards have included 6 D&AD Silver nominations, Campaign Press Gold & Silvers, British Television Silvers, a Eurobest Gold, Cannes Gold and a Cannes Silver. She was made a Board Director of BBH and Creative Group Head in 1990. She is still married to Peter with whom she has 2 wonderful boys aged 2 and 4.

PAUL BIDDLE – Paul Biddle specialises in Advertising, Design, Still-life and Photo-illustration, plus a small amount of Editorial and Publishing work. Paul has won a number of photographic awards including a Gold and Merit in 1989, and a Merit in 1990 in our very own Association Awards, a Gold in 1991 and 1992 for the R.P.S., a Kodak Triple Exposure in 1991, and for the 3D New Illustrators Awards a Bronze in 1993 and a Gold and 7 Bronzes in 1994.

DAVE BUONAGUIDI – Dave Buonaguidi is joint Creative Director at St. Luke's. He works mainly in advertising and occasionally in design work when required by clients. His claims to fame are knowing Zodiac from the Gladiators and playing cricket for Italy.

PAUL CARBERRY – Paul Carberry is a Creative Partner working in through the line integrated marketing.

CHRIS CHEETHAM – Chris Cheetham works mainly in advertising and location photography and has been a winner of various AFAEP Awards from 1985 onwards. His personal work has now started appearing in various private and corporate collections.

GILL DAVIES – Gill Davies is a founding director of Tatham Pearce and has experience working in corporate identity, corporate and product brochures, and annual reports. She began her career working for Alan Fletcher at Pentagram Design, moving on to become Art Director of Reader's Digest in Cape Town. She regularly commissions and art directs photographs for clients including Barclays Bank, Granada Group and Sea Containers. Gill is a member of the Design & Art Directors' Association and the Chartered Society of Designers. She has judged the British Environment and Media Awards and is a founder member and former vice chair of Women in Marketing and Design.

GARY HOLT – Gary Holt graduated from university with a 1st Class Honours Degree in Graphic Design in 1990. During his time at college he worked at CDT and went on to work full-time at Lambie-Nairn (sister company to Tutssels) on leaving college. He is now a designer at Tutssels where his main areas of work include TV corporate, corporate, literature and multi-media design, in the UK and across Europe. He regularly commissions and art directs photography across a range of products and has also been involved in motion control. His major clients include BBC and BBC World, Carlton Television, Bravo, Ka 2 (Belgium), TvNorge (Norway), ARTE (France & Germany), RTSI (Switzerland), BT and Boots. He won a BPME Award for his work on Bravo.

KIKI KENDRICK – Kiki Kendrick works as an Art Director at Abbott Mead Vickers BBDO where she also claims to be official first aider and birthday cake maker for the 7th floor. Her main areas of work are press, poster and TV advertising. She has worked a lot on women's products which she says she loves doing but is dying to do a campaign for the Vegetarian Society or Animal Rights. She has had work in 'The Book' a few times, plus Bronze and Silver awards for Campaign Press & Poster and British Telly. Kiki worked in New York for two years, returning last October. The 'always a bridesmaid never the bride' scenario all changed when she was a Blind Date contestant this year and got picked. She always wears something shocking, a silly hat, an animated hair-do, and claims to drive the most famous car in London.

PETER MARLOW – Photo-journalist Peter Marlow, joined Magnum Photos in 1981 and was the president of Magnum between 1990-1993. He was the curator of the recent 'George Rodger Retrospective' exhibition at the Barbican Art Gallery. A book of his work, 'Liverpool - Looking out to Sea', was published by Cape in 1993.

CAROLINE METCALFE – Having worked at The Observer from 1981-87, Caroline Metcalfe joined the Independent Magazine at its launch in 1988 and is currently the Picture Editor for the Independent Saturday Magazine. Her main areas of work are commissioning photography, editing and viewing new portfolios. She has been the UK Co-ordinator for the World Press Photo Competition and Exhibition since 1989.

PETER ROBINSON – Having studied Engineering at University, Peter Robinson became a freelance photographer in 1965 and spent two years travelling through Asia. Peter worked as a photojournalist in London and New York, but became a full time sports photographer after being commissioned to shoot the 1972 Olympic Games. In 1994, in conjunction with The Observer, he curated an exhibition at The Association Gallery, "This is Soccer", an alternative look at The 1994 World Cup Championships. He has recently completed a Masters Degree at The Royal College of Art, his subject – Interactive Multi Media.

CHARLES SETTRINGTON – As well as working as an advertising photographer, Charles Settrington is also the Managing Director of the Goodwood Group of companies, comprising the house, race course, aerodrome and motor circuit. For the past three years Charles has become more involved at Goodwood. In this time he has created the Goodwood Festival of Speed, which has become the biggest Classic Car event in the world. Charles' first job however, was working for Stanley Kubrick on the film 'Barry Lyndon'. He was also the first person to work with heavily painted two-dimensional trompe l'oeil sets. Charles also created the Osborne & Little advertising campaign of which one image is in the permanent collection of advertising photography in the Centre Pompidou, Paris.

GEOFF SMITH – Geoff Smith's specialities as a photographer are people and fashion/location. Having originally worked in Manchester, he is now based in London. Geoff was mentioned in the First AFAEP Awards and his claim to fame is knowing Martin Beckett before he was famous.

MALCOLM VENVILLE – Director and photographer.

PAUL WEBSTER – Paul Webster grew up in Blackpool. He studied Graphic Design at the college there, followed by a Post Grad in Typographic Design at the LCP. After a varied career in general graphic and magazine design, he started working at Sainsbury's The Magazine in 1993 as Art Director. He has enjoyed seeing the magazine rise in circulation to 350,000 and is looking forward to the company expanding into other areas of publishing.

Once again, Fuji Professional are delighted to be sponsoring the Association Awards - regarded as the indicator of quality within the British photographic industry. Supporting the work of the Association of Photographers is important to Fuji Professional and our level of commitment is demonstrated through a variety of initiatives.

Now in its second year, Fuji Art is building on the success of last year and is actively promoting creation of non-commissioned photography. We have also strengthened our support for Assistants by backing a new series of seminars and lectures as well as facilitating a 24 hour job board outside the Association Gallery. We are also continuing our sponsorship of the now highly prestigious Assistants' Awards and the production of the accompanying catalogue, now in its second year.

Fujifilm's commitment to photography and innovation is perhaps best displayed within its range of world renowned photographic products and imaging solutions. We are proud to be able to support the professional photographic industry through our technological developments, training and marketing support.

GRAHAM RUTHERFORD
Divisional Manager – Fuji Professional Photographic Division

sponsored by

Photographer: GILES REVELL
Printer: JOHN BETTELL
Awarded: **GOLD**

Photographer: AERNOUT OVERBEEKE
Printer: AERNOUT OVERBEEKE
Title: WATER RESISTANT BATHING SUIT, ARUBA
Awarded: **SILVER**

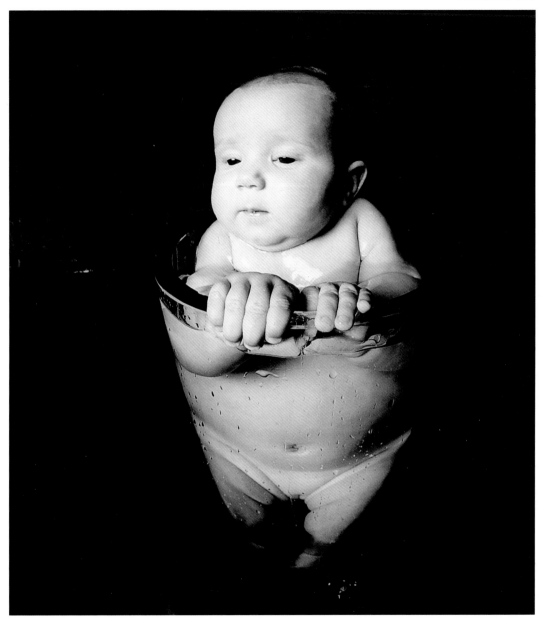

Photographer: TONY MAY
Printer: THE GREAT RON BAGLEY
Title: ELOISE, 4 MONTHS 4 DAYS
Awarded: **MERIT**

Photographer: STUART REDLER
Printer: STUART REDLER

Photographer: RICARDO ALCAIDE
Printer: PETER GUEST

Photographer: DAVID STEWART
Printer: SIMON BELL
Client: "CABBAGE"
Art Director: TONY VEAZEY
Hair & Make-up: LAURA FRANKUM
Casting & Styling: SUE ODELL
Model-maker: WESLEY WEST

Photographer: RAY MASSEY
Printer: MASTER MONO
Title: EQUILIBRISTS: ERNESTO & KATIE SARABIA, MIMESCOPE

Photographer: CARL WARNER
Printer: MIKE AT LIGHTHOUSE

Photographer: RICARDO ALCAIDE
Printer: PETER GUEST

As Europe's leading manufacturer of high quality photographic equipment and materials, Agfa are delighted to support The Association of Photographers Awards once again in this, their thirteenth year.

Through our sponsorship of the Personal Landscape category, Agfa welcome a unique opportunity to salute proven excellence in the challenging field of professional photography.

Our focus on the needs of the demanding professional is, as always, wide and far-reaching. Agfa are dedicated to the continual development of land-mark products that we hope will help expand your creative horizons.

PIERRE MULLER
Group Product Manager, Professional – AGFA

sponsored by

Photographer: AERNOUT OVERBEEKE
Printer: AERNOUT OVERBEEKE
Title: REJECTED CRANE, ALESUND, NORWAY
Awarded: **MERIT**

Photographer: CHRIS SIMPSON
C Type Printer: STEVE BARNES AT THE COLOUR CENTRE
Iris Printer: GEORGE WALFALL AT TAPESTRY
Art Director: CHRIS SIMPSON
Title: DRY STONE WALL, THE LAKE DISTRICT

Photographer: ROBERT WALKER
Printer: MAT WRIGHT
Title: KAZAN, RUSSIA

Photographer: ADRI BERGER
Printer: ADRI BERGER
Title: RED SQUARE, MOSCOW

Photographer: JOHN OFFENBACH
Printer: JOHN OFFENBACH

Photographer: AERNOUT OVERBEEKE
Printer: AERNOUT OVERBEEKE
Title: RAVEN ABOVE DEATH VALLEY, USA

Photographer: RICHARD CLARK
Printer: RICHARD CLARK

Photographer: SHAUN HIGSON
Printer: SHAUN HIGSON

Photographer: MICHAEL FEATHER (Assistant Member)
Printer: MICHAEL FEATHER
Title: VIANO DO CASTELO, PORTUGAL

Photographer: GEORGE KAVANAGH
Printer: KLAUS KALDE

Photographer: CHRIS SIMPSON
Printer: MIKE AT LIGHTHOUSE
Art Director: CHRIS SIMPSON
Title: GLACIER NATIONAL PARK, MONTANA

Photographer: JUSTIN PUMFREY
Printer: JUSTIN PUMFREY

Photographer: PETE SEAWARD
Printer: MALCOLM PASLEY

Continuing our commitment to championing the alliance between the art of photography and the science of digital imaging, Dicomed is again proud to sponsor The Association of Photographers Thirteenth Awards.

For 27 years, Dicomed Inc. has pioneered digital imaging systems to a wide range of creative individuals. This year's release of the "BigShot" full format, high resolution, digital back for the Hasselblad brings, for the first time, "Digital Photography without Compromise" to the professional photographer.

TREVOR HAWORTH
President & CEO – Dicomed Inc

sponsored by

Photographer: DAVID STEWART
Printer: JEAN LOCK AT VISIONS
Client: "CABBAGE"
Costume: MANDY GOLDSMITH
Casting: SUE ODELL
Model-maker: WESLEY WEST

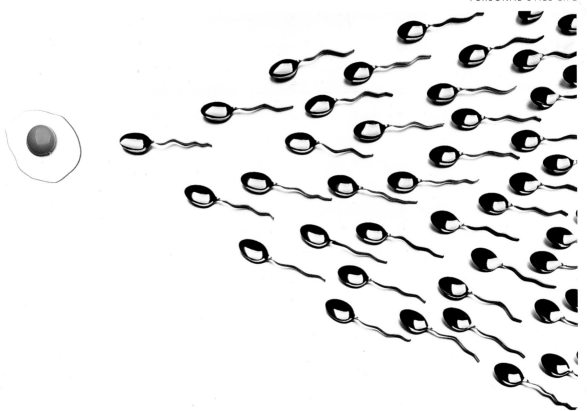

Photographer: MARK POLYBLANK
Printer: JEAN LOCK AT VISIONS

Photographer: MARC BURDEN
Printer: MATCHLESS

Photographer: ANDY WORNELL
Printer: ANDY WORNELL

It is, as always, a pleasure to support The Awards.

We again sponsor the Personal Manipulation section, an area we have been very active in over the last two years.

Our aim has been to provide the facilities for photographers to come to terms with this new technology and then to support their needs as they put their new skills to creative and commercial use.

We whole-heartedly support the enthusiasm and technical excellence illustrated on the following pages, and will continue to be dedicated to supporting the art of the photographer.

BEN RICHARDSON
Managing Director – Metro Imaging Ltd

sponsored by

M e T r O

Photographer: COLIN THOMAS
Printer: METRO
System Operator: COLIN THOMAS
Stylist: GLYNIS COX
Make-up Artist: KATHERINE ROSS

Photographer: PHIL CAWLEY
Printer: METRO
System Operator: PHIL CAWLEY

Photographer: NICK GEORGHIOU
Printer: NICK GEORGHIOU

Photographer: SIMON SOMERVILLE
Printers: RICHARD & OLLIE AT KEISHI PRINT
System Operator: GARY & JOHN AT COLOURSPACE
Art Directors: SIMON SOMERVILLE & RICHARD SLITHAN
Make-up: CLAIRE RAY
Model: CLAIRE PORTER
Awarded: **MERIT**

Photographer: SIMON SOMERVILLE
Printers: RICHARD & OLLIE AT KEISHI PRINT
System Operator: GARY & JOHN AT COLOURSPACE
Art Directors: SIMON SOMERVILLE & RICHARD SLITHAN
Make-up: CLAIRE RAY
Model: CLAIRE PORTER
Awarded: **MERIT**

Photographer: JONATHAN ROOT
Printer: DIRECT COLOUR
Stylist: MAXIME SIWAN
Hair & Make-up: DARREN EVANS
Title: ENFANTS TERRIBLES
Awarded: **MERIT**

Photographer: JONATHAN ROOT
Printer: DIRECT COLOUR
Stylist: MAXIME SIWAN
Hair & Make-up: DARREN EVANS
Title: ENFANTS TERRIBLES
Awarded: **MERIT**

Photographer: CHRIS SIMPSON
Iris Prints: GEORGE WALFALL AT TAPESTRY
Art Director: CHRIS SIMPSON

Photographer: CHRIS SIMPSON
Iris Prints: GEORGE WALFALL AT TAPESTRY
Art Director: CHRIS SIMPSON

Photographer: ANDREAS HEUMANN
Iris Prints: ANDREAS HEUMANN

Photographer: ANDREAS HEUMANN
Iris Prints: ANDREAS HEUMANN

Photographer: KEVIN KINGSTON
Printer: BRIAN DOWLING AT B.D.I.

Photographer: KEVIN KINGSTON
Printer: BRIAN DOWLING AT B.D.I.

In 1995, Olympus supported two exhibitions in the Association Gallery, helped to organise a photographic car rally for members, spent three days on the road with them discovering that they drink like fish and take damn good photographs. And once again here we are in this book having gathered up the funds to back these prestigious awards.

I guess it clearly illustrates that Olympus are avid supporters of the Association and what it stands for. Long may these Awards continue and long live the success of the individuals who bring stimulating photography to the eyes of the nation.

IAN DICKENS
Communications Director – Olympus

sponsored by

Photographer: ROLPH GOBITS
Printer: ROLPH GOBITS
Awarded: **SILVER**

Photographer: ROLPH GOBITS
Printer: ROLPH GOBITS
Awarded: **SILVER**

Photographer: RICARDO ALCAIDE
Printer: PETER GUEST
Awarded: **MERIT**

Photographer: RICARDO ALCAIDE
Printer: PETER GUEST
Awarded: **MERIT**

Photographer: NICK GEORGHIOU
Printer: NICK GEORGHIOU
Title: RATTING ON A PIG FARM
Awarded: **MERIT**

Photographer: NICK GEORGHIOU
Printer: NICK GEORGHIOU
Title: RATTING ON A PIG FARM
Awarded: **MERIT**

Photographer: NICK GEORGHIOU
Printer: NICK GEORGHIOU
Title: RATTING ON DEK'S PEN

Photographer: NICK GEORGHIOU
Printer: NICK GEORGHIOU
Title: RATTING ON DEK'S PEN

Photographer: JANE HILTON
Printer: ROBERTO

Photographer: JANE HILTON
Printer: ROBERTO

Photographer: MARK POLYBLANK
Printer: TONY WHITE
Costume made by: KATE MALCOLM

Photographer: MARK POLYBLANK
Printer: TONY WHITE
Costume made by: KATE MALCOLM (left)
Costume styling: KATE MALCOLM (right)

We have become used to hearing The Awards referred to as the 'Oscars' of photography. Whilst this conveys the prestige they now hold, I doubt that the 'Oscars' inspire, surprise and challenge their Industry in quite the same way. For those reasons, I believe The Awards stand apart - rather like 'Melinex' from ICI.

Supergloss prints based on 'Melinex' give a surface gloss, flatness, enhanced colour saturation and definition of detail which shows your work to its best advantage - time after time.

'Melinex' is delighted to continue its association with The Awards and offers its congratulations to the organisers and entrants who have contributed to the success of The Awards over recent years.

DAVID MACLEOD
Managing Director – 'Melinex' Europe

sponsored by

Photographer: DAVID STEWART
Printer: JEAN LOCK AT VISIONS
Client: KINGFISHER TOOTHPASTE
Commissioned by: BROADBENT CHEETHAM VEAZEY
Art Director: TONY VEAZEY & MIKE KEANE
Casting/Props: WESLEY WEST
Awarded: **SILVER**

Photographer: PHILIP LEE HARVEY
Printer: JEAN LOCK AT VISIONS
Client: KODAK
Commissioned by: MATRIX
Art Director: DAVE WOODCOCK
Awarded: **MERIT**

Photographer: DARRAN REES
Printer: JEAN LOCK AT VISIONS
Client: SUN ALLIANCE
Commissioned by: LEAGAS SHAFRON DAVIS
Art Director: STEVE GRIME
System Operator: TAPESTRY
Production Assistant: KATE EVANS, MUGSHOTS

Photographer: PAUL REES
Client: SUN ALLIANCE
Commissioned by: LEAGAS SHAFRON DAVIS
Art Directors: ROB JANOWSKI & STEVE GRIME

Photographer: MARTIN BECKETT
Printer: MIKE DAVIS AT METRO
Client: VOLVO
Commissioned by: WWAV RAPP COLLINS
Art Director: MARK MUGGERIDGE
System Operator: GANDEE AT METRO

Photographer: MAX FORSYTHE
Printer: PHIL HOLDING AT PUSH ONE
Client: HUSH PUPPIES
Commissioned by: YOUNG & RUBICAM
Art Director: GRAEME NORWAYS

Photographer: MARTIN BECKETT
Printer: MIKE DAVIS AT METRO
Client: VOLVO
Commissioned by: WWAV RAPP COLLINS
Art Director: MARK MUGGERIDGE
System Operator: GANDEE AT METRO

Photographer: MAX FORSYTHE
Printer: PHIL HOLDING AT PUSH ONE
Client: HUSH PUPPIES
Commissioned by: YOUNG & RUBICAM
Art Director: GRAEME NORWAYS

Once again ILFORD are delighted to sponsor the Commissioned Advertising Black & White category of The Awards.

Black and white continues to be an important part of the competition and our company is committed to providing our customers with a wide range of film, paper and chemicals for monochrome work.

While ILFORD is best known for its traditional black and white products the Ilfochrome range of reversal materials remains important and 1996 will see the launch of our own range of ink jet consumables under the name of Ilfojet, for the fast growing digital market.

Our congratulations to all the winners of The Thirteenth Awards.

BILL TIMMIS

Marketing and Planning Manager – ILFORD

sponsored by

Photographer: MARTIN BECKETT
Printer: KEITH TAYLOR
Client: VOLVO
Commissioned by: WWAV RAPP COLLINS
Art Director: MARK MUGGERIDGE
Awarded: **MERIT**

Photographer: MARTIN BECKETT
Printer: KEITH TAYLOR
Client: VOLVO
Commissioned by: WWAV RAPP COLLINS
Art Director: MARK MUGGERIDGE

Photographer: KIRAN MASTER
Printer: LIGHTHOUSE
Client: C.O.I.
Commissioned by: LEAGAS SHAFRON DAVIS
Art Director: STEVE GRIME
Stylist: JANE FIELD
Hair & Make-up: JULIE DARTNELL

Photographer: SIMON STOCK
Printer: MIKE AT LIGHTHOUSE
Client: SUN ALLIANCE
Commissioned by: LEAGAS SHAFRON DAVIS
Art Director: STEVE CAMPBELL
Model Maker: ACK ACK

Photographer: SIMON STOCK
Printer: MIKE AT LIGHTHOUSE
Client: NATIONWIDE
Commissioned by: GGT
Art Director: ERIK KESSELS
Casting: MUGSHOTS

Photographer: JAN CHLEBIK
Printer: MARSHALL WALKER
Client: FMC CORPORATION (UK) LTD PROCESS ADDITIVES DIVISION
Commissioned by: THE CREATIVE LYNX PARTNERSHIP
Art Director: STUART WILSON
Title: VENICE

Photographer: HENRIK THORUP KNUDSEN
Printer: HENRIK THORUP KNUDSEN
Client: IDV/PIAT
Commissioned by: BURKITT EDWARDS MARTIN
Art Director: PAUL SIMBLETT

Photographer: LEON
Printer: LEON
Client: NATIONAL CANINE DEFENCE LEAGUE
Commissioned by: TBWA
Art Director: STEVE CHETHAM
Creative Director: TREVOR BEATTIE
Model: TROTSKY

Photographer: LAURENCE HASKELL
Printer: LAURENCE HASKELL
Client: PEPE
Commissioned by: LEAGAS DELANEY

Photographer: HENRIK THORUP KNUDSEN
Printer: HENRIK THORUP KNUDSEN & QUICKSILVER
Client: EPS/EUROSTAR
Commissioned by: YOUNG & RUBICAM
Art Director: BRIAN CONNOLLY
System Operator: HENRIK THORUP KNUDSEN/CETA IMAGING

The paper industry that was fearful of the computer screen, now produces more paper.

The tunnel has stimulated and improved the quality of cross-channel travel by sea.

Similarly, a record number of accepted entries into the 13th Awards of The Association of Photographers indicates that the spirit of creative photographers has not been dampened by new technology, but rekindled.

1995 witnessed metamorphosis at Primary Colour to keep pace with this new energy. We are proud to offer our continued support to The Association, its members and the Industry in general.

BRIAN DE KRETZER
Primary Colour

sponsored by

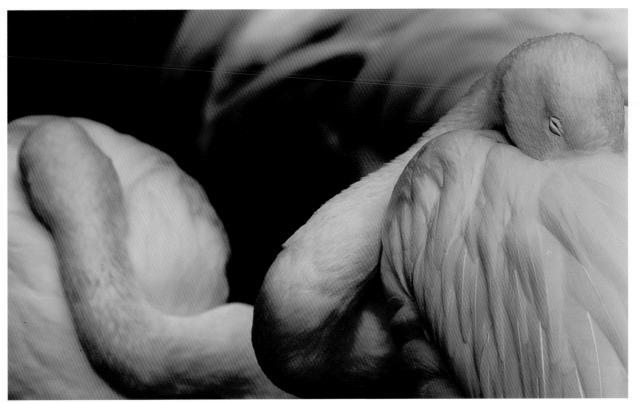

Photographer: JEAN-LUC BENARD
Printer: JOHN AIREY AT DIRECT COLOUR
Client: LONDON ZOO
Commissioned by: ADDISON DESIGN
Art Director: GRAHAM TAYLOR
Awarded: **SILVER**

Photographer: ULI WEBER
Printer: BRIAN AT B.D.I.
Client: SUNDAY TIMES MAGAZINE
Commissioned by: KIM ANDREOLLI
Art Director: PEDRO SILMON
Title: KYLIE MINOGUE

101

Photographer: BARRY MARSDEN
Printer: GODFREY AT JOE'S BASEMENT
Client: VOX
Commissioned by: PAUL AARONS
Art Director: PAUL AARONS
Title: JARVIS COCKER

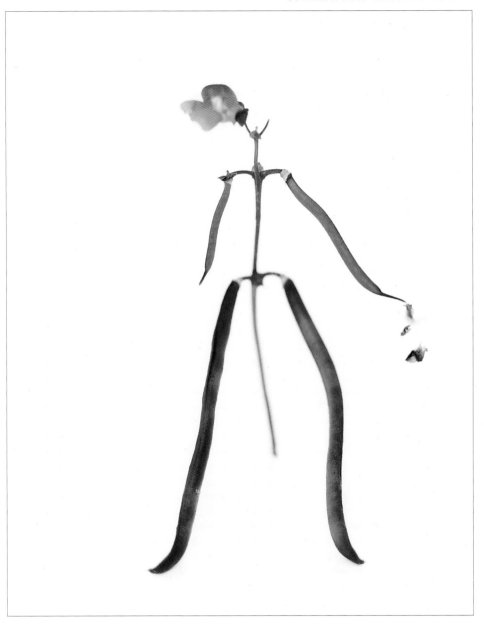

Photographer: SIMON BROWN
Printer: VISIONS
Client: HOUSE & GARDEN MAGAZINE

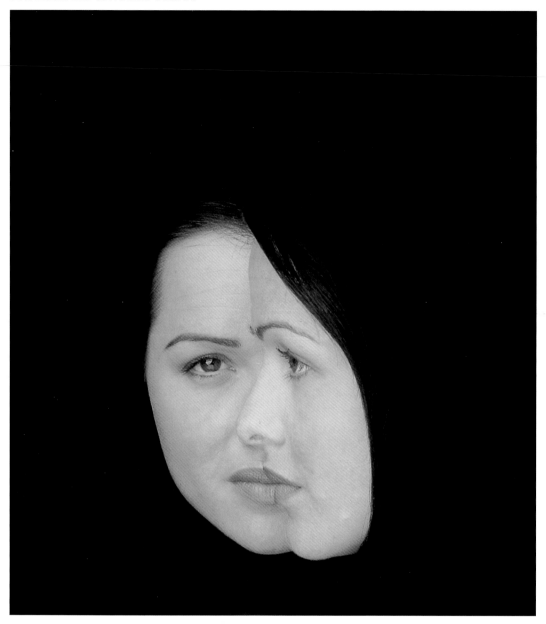

Photographer: TIM O'SULLIVAN
Printer: DANNY POPE
Client: NIGHT & DAY MAGAZINE
Commissioned by: TIM LEITH

Photographer: ROBIN BROADBENT
Printer: QUICKSILVER
Client: KEW MAGAZINE
Commissioned by: ESTERSON LACKERSTEEN
Art Director: MIKE LACKERSTEEN

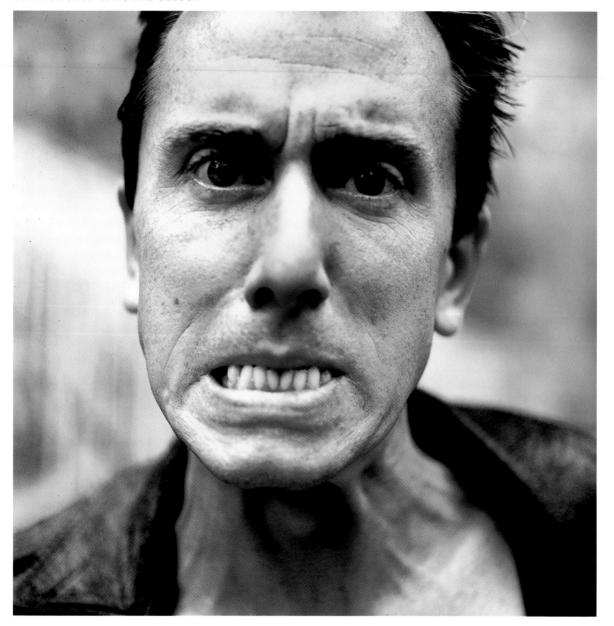

Photographer: ULI WEBER
Printer: BRIAN AT B.D.I.
Client: SUNDAY TIMES MAGAZINE
Commissioned by: KIM ANDREOLLI
Art Director: PEDRO SILMON
Title: TIM ROTH

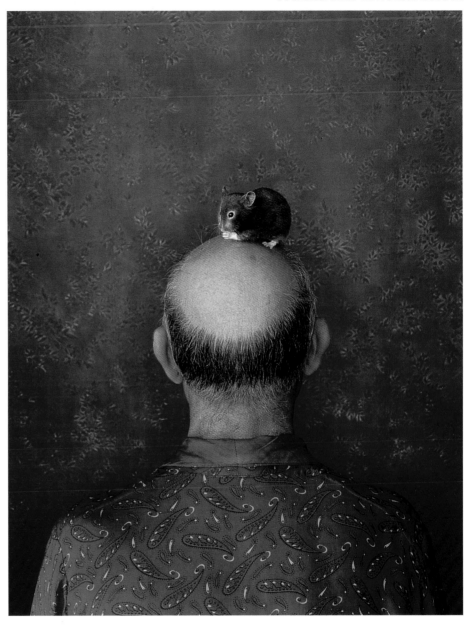

Photographer: SARA MORRIS
Printer: DANNY POPE
Client: JONATHAN CAPE BOOKS
Art Director: CHRIS SHAMWANA

My belief in the Association as a catalyst for creative talent never waivers and in fact is strengthened each year when we see the standard of creativity, skill and imagination laid before us.

As always our thanks goes to the AOP for their unstinting dedication and hard work. It is our pleasure to support them and give something back to an industry which has always supported us.

GREGG FORTE
Managing Director – Joe's Basement Ltd

sponsored by

Photographer: ADRIAN COOK
Printer: ADRIAN COOK
Client: WHITEWATER RECORDS
Commissioned by: TESSA STURRIDGE
Print distresser: LIAM NEARY
Styling: JANE FIELD
Awarded: **MERIT**

Photographer: TIF HUNTER
Printer: TIF HUNTER
Client: THE INDEPENDENT
Awarded: **MERIT**

Photographer: MARCUS LYON
Printer: JOHN RAY BETTELL
Client: RED
Commissioned by: CARL GRINTER
Art Director: IAN BRYERS

Photographer: ADRIAN COOK
Printer: ADRIAN COOK
Client: WHITEWATER RECORDS
Commissioned by: TESSA STURRIDGE
Print distresser: LIAM NEARY
Styling: JANE FIELD

Photographer: DOD MILLER
Printer: MIKE SPRY AT DOWNTOWN DARKROOM
Client: INDEPENDENT ON SUNDAY MAGAZINE
Commissioned by: VICTORIA LUKENS
Title: COW JUDGING AT PETERBORO' AGRICULTURAL FAIR

Photographer: GILES REVELL
Printer: JOHN BETTELL
Client: BIG MAGAZINE
Commissioned by: VINCE FROST
Art Director: VINCE FROST
Title: DAVE, DELIVERENCE COURIERS

Photographer: WENDY CARRIG
Printer: STEVE WALSH AT DOWNTOWN DARKROOM
Client: IRISH TATLER
Commissioned by: MORAG PRUNTY
Styling: LAURA BACHARACH
Hair & Make-up: HELEN WALSH

Photographer: SIMON HARSENT
Client: CLUB 21
Commissioned by: CLUB 21
Art Director: CHRIS CHEONG

Photographer: TESSA TRAEGER
Printer: TONY WHITE
Client: FESTIVAL DES ARTS, ST AGRÈVE
Commissioned by: PAUL BOUCHER
Art Director: PATRICK KINMONTH

"Tapestry, they're a good old firm. Got us out of trouble many a time".

ALAN WALDIE

Vice Chairman – Lowe Howard Spink

(Guest presenter 1995 Association Awards)

sponsored by

TAPESTRY

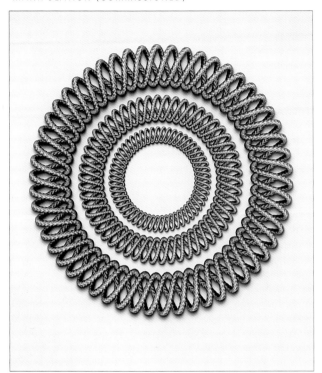

Photographer: GILES REVELL
Client: SAVOY GROUP HOTELS
Commissioned by: PENTAGRAM
Art Directors: JOHN RUSHWORTH & GILES REVELL
System Operator: GILES REVELL
Awarded: **SILVER**

Photographer: GILES REVELL
Client: SAVOY GROUP HOTELS
Commissioned by: PENTAGRAM
Art Directors: JOHN RUSHWORTH & GILES REVELL
System Operator: GILES REVELL
Awarded: **SILVER**

Photographer: ANDREAS HEUMANN
Printer: ANDREAS HEUMANN
Client: IDV (UK) LTD SMIRNOFF VODKA
Commissioned by: LOWE HOWARD SPINK
Art Director: COLIN LAMBERTON
System Operator: ANDREAS HEUMANN
Awarded: **MERIT**

Photographer: TIM FLACH
Printer: KEITH TAYLOR AT METRO
Client: KODAK OFFICE IMAGING
Commissioned by: BANKS & ZIEJA LTD
Art Director: LEN THOMSON
System Operator: BERNI AT ALCHEMY CREATIVE SERVICES
Model Maker: TIM FLACH
Background Artist: SIMON BRINGLE

Photographer: LEWIS MULATERO
Printer: METRO
Client: THE COCA-COLA COMPANY
Commissioned by: CHIAT DAY
Art Director: ERIC HOUSEKNECHT
System Operator: MARK DEAMER-SMITH, CASHMAN BORKITT

Photographer: LEWIS MULATERO
Printer: METRO
Client: THE COCA-COLA COMPANY
Commissioned by: CHIAT DAY
Art Director: ERIC HOUSEKNECHT
System Operator: MARK DEAMER-SMITH, CASHMAN BORKITT

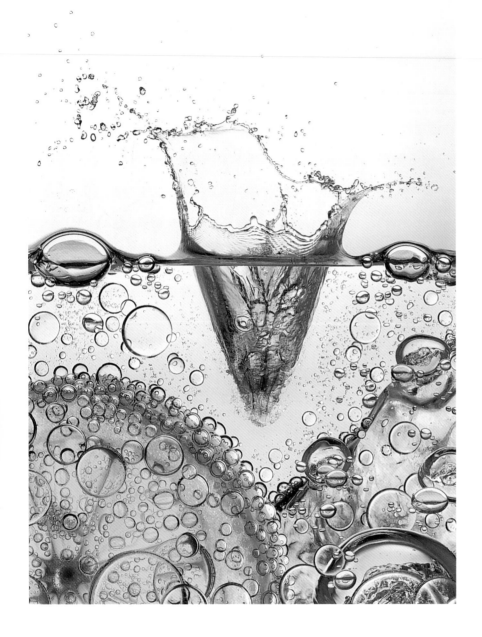

Photographer: BARRY LATEGAN
Client: GORDON'S GIN
Commissioned by: LEO BURNETT
Art Director: MARK TUTSSEL
System Operator: DAN TIERNEY
Effects: ANDY KNIGHT

Photographer: TIM O'SULLIVAN
Printer: DANNY POPE
Client: OBSERVER LIFE MAGAZINE
Commissioned by: NICK HALL
System Operator: JOHN WHILLOCK

Photographer: DAVID STEWART
Printer: JEAN LOCK AT VISIONS
Client: CAMELOT
Commissioned by: SAATCHI & SAATCHI
Art Directors: PAUL TAYLOR & BILL GALLACHER
System Operator: THE COLOUR COMPANY – TONY MOXHAY & JOHN SWIFT
Casting & Styling: SUE ODELL
Model Maker: WESLEY WEST
Hair & Make-up: LAURA FRANKUM

Photographer: DAVID STEWART
Printer: JEAN LOCK AT VISIONS
Client: CAMELOT
Commissioned by: SAATCHI & SAATCHI
Art Directors: PAUL TAYLOR & BILL GALLACHER
System Operator: THE COLOUR COMPANY – TONY MOXHAY & JOHN SWIFT
Casting & Styling: SUE ODELL
Plaster Man Styling: JANE FIELD
Model Maker: WESLEY WEST
Hair & Make-up: LAURA FRANKUM

Photographer: BARRY LATEGAN
Client: GORDON'S GIN
Commissioned by: LEO BURNETT
Art Director: MARK TUTSSEL
System Operator: DAN TIERNEY
Effects: ANDY KNIGHT

The essence of the most outstanding photography in the world is its inherent creativity.

Polaroid is proud to support such creativity in the guise of 'P' magazine which features some of the most artistic work originated on Polaroid materials.

We are pleased that the new 'Creative Art' section of The Awards has attracted work of an equally creative and artistic nature.

CHARLIE YIANOULLOU
European Sector Manager – Professional Photography

sponsored by

Photographer: ROBERT WALKER
Printer: MAT WRIGHT
Client: GARRETT & CO
Commissioned by: THE CHASE
Art Director: RICHARD SCHOLEY

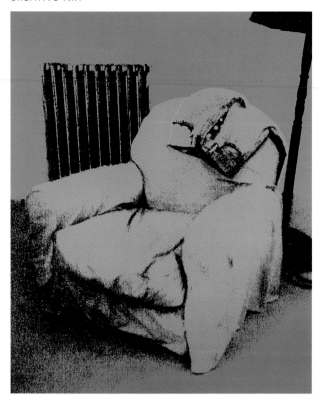
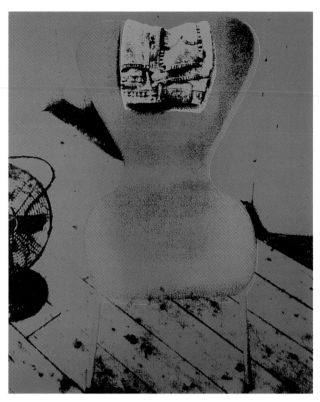

Photographer: JOHN OFFENBACH
Client: LEVIS
Commissioned by: BARTLE BOGLE HEGARTY
Art Director: RUSSEL RAMSEY
Title: "LOOSE", "GIRLS"

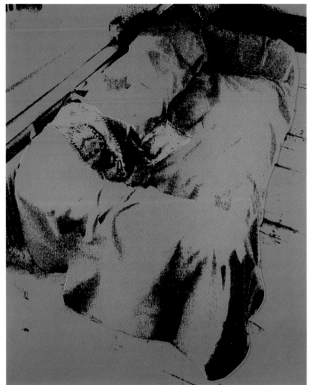

Photographer: JOHN OFFENBACH
Client: LEVIS
Commissioned by: BARTLE BOGLE HEGARTY
Art Director: RUSSEL RAMSEY
Title: "REGULAR", "SUPER LOOSE"

Ceta Services Ltd. is now into its 25th year. The company is now three labs strong, located in Kensington, Poland Street in the West End of London and in the City Financial District. CETA's colour processing quality is legendary amongst the leading fashion, advertising and fine art photographers. CETA attribute their success to its highly trained loyal staff, providing a top quality personal service.

At the Poland Street lab, in addition to E6 processing, CETA offers a wide selection of colour printing and processing services, reproduction quality duplicates and black & white hand printing.

FILMS Ltd. delivers professional films of every make twice daily to all studios and users in London, supplying all leading makes of colour film, black & white paper, chemicals etc.

CETA Electronic Imaging is the latest addition to their services and is the first Dicomed Imaging Service Centre in London, offering high end top quality Scanning and Outputs. Specialising in outputing high quality reproduction transparencies from the high resolution Dicomed Digital Camera which is the world leader in this technology. CETA offers hardware packages with the latest Dicomed Imaginator 5.0 software, specially written for professional photographers.

STEVE KENT

Managing Director – CETA Services Ltd

sponsored by

Photographer: JONATHAN ROOT
Printer: DIRECT COLOUR
Client: EVENING STANDARD
Hair & Make-up: DARREN EVANS
Stylist: SOPHIA NEOPHITOU
Title: TWINS IN TWINSETS
Awarded: **SILVER**

Photographer: JONATHAN ROOT
Printer: DIRECT COLOUR
Client: EVENING STANDARD
System Operator: TAPESTRY (right)
Hair & Make-up: DARREN EVANS
Stylist: SOPHIA NEOPHITOU
Title: TWINS IN TWINSETS
Awarded: **SILVER**

Photographer: NADAV KANDER
Printer: BRIAN DOWLING
Client: MARLBORO
Commissioned by: BAINSFAIR SHARKEY TROTT
Art Directors: PAUL LEEVES & LEE GOULDING
Awarded: **MERIT**

Photographer: NADAV KANDER
Printer: BRIAN DOWLING (top)
Printer: DENNIS WATSON (bottom)
Client: MARLBORO
Commissioned by: BAINSFAIR SHARKEY TROTT
Art Directors: PAUL LEEVES & LEE GOULDING
Awarded: **MERIT**

Photographer: PETER DAZELEY
Printer: PHIL HOLDING AT PUSH ONE
Client: BTEC
Commissioned by: CHATLAND SAYER
Art Director: NIGEL CHATLAND
Awarded: **MERIT**

Photographer: PETER DAZELEY
Printer: PHIL HOLDING AT PUSH ONE
Client: BTEC
Commissioned by: CHATLAND SAYER
Art Director: NIGEL CHATLAND
Awarded: **MERIT**

Photographer: DAVID SCHEINMANN
Printer: METRO
Client: IBM
Commissioned by: OGILVY & MATHER, PARIS
Art Director: MARCUS FERNANDEZ
System Operator: DAN TIERNEY

Photographer: DAVID SCHEINMANN
Printer: METRO
Client: IBM
Commissioned by: OGILVY & MATHER, PARIS
Art Director: MARCUS FERNANDEZ
System Operator: DAN TIERNEY

In the past twelve months Calumet International Group, operating companies in America and mainland Europe have enjoyed an increasing level of business with AOP members on their travels, and look forward to providing even greater choice and wider international presence in the year ahead.

In the UK, KJP has continued its successful expansion programme with the total refurbishment of its flagship showroom in London, a major extension in Manchester to create the largest professional showroom in the North, new showrooms in Croydon, Liverpool and Leeds, and the latest addition to the group with the recent opening of Glasgow,

bringing our UK network to a total of 16. All this combines to make KJP the professionals' first choice, not only for its unparalleled choice of stocked products, but also for its tremendous range of facilities, services and support.

KJP are firmly committed to continue sponsorship of The Awards as well as to supporting members' ongoing success in keeping their work in the vanguard of world class images.

STUART WALLACE
Group Marketing Director – KJP
(part of the Calumet International Group)

sponsored by

Photographer: ALLAN GRAINGER
Printer: ALLAN GRAINGER
Client: ALLIANCE & LEICESTER
Commissioned by: BMP DDB NEEDHAM
Art Directors: PETER GATLEY & TONY DAVIDSON
Awarded: **SILVER**

Photographer: ALLAN GRAINGER
Printer: ALLAN GRAINGER
Client: ALLIANCE & LEICESTER
Commissioned by: BMP DDB NEEDHAM
Art Directors: PETER GATLEY & TONY DAVIDSON
Awarded: **SILVER**

Photographer: DOD MILLER
Printer: MIKE SPRY AT DOWNTOWN DARKROOM
Client: THE INDEPENDENT MAGAZINE
Title: BOGNOR BIRDMEN
Awarded: **MERIT**

Photographer: DOD MILLER
Printer: MIKE SPRY AT DOWNTOWN DARKROOM
Client: THE INDEPENDENT MAGAZINE
Title: BOGNOR BIRDMEN
Awarded: **MERIT**

Photographer: CHRIS HARRISON
Printer: GARY WILSON
Client: THE INDEPENDENT MAGAZINE
Commissioned by: COLIN JACOBSON
Title: ROYAL MARINE SNIPERS
Awarded: **MERIT**

Photographer: CHRIS HARRISON
Printer: GARY WILSON
Client: THE INDEPENDENT MAGAZINE
Commissioned by: COLIN JACOBSON
Title: ROYAL MARINE SNIPERS
Awarded: **MERIT**

Photographer: ROBERT WALKER
Printer: MAT WRIGHT
Client: GARRETT & CO
Commissioned by: THE CHASE
Art Director: RICHARD SCHOLEY
Model Maker: SUSAN WALKER
Awarded: **MERIT**

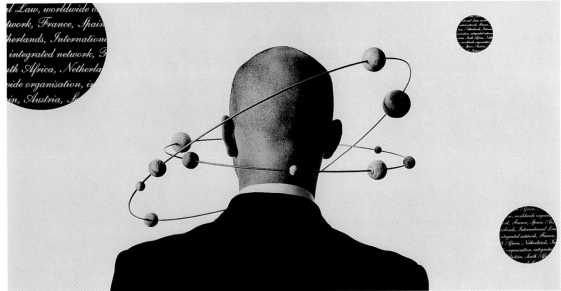

Photographer: ROBERT WALKER
Printer: MAT WRIGHT
Client: GARRETT & CO
Commissioned by: THE CHASE
Art Director: RICHARD SCHOLEY
Model Maker: SUSAN WALKER
Awarded: **MERIT**

Photographer: DOD MILLER
Printer: MIKE SPRY AT DOWNTOWN DARKROOM
Client: OBSERVER LIFE MAGAZINE
Title: SMOKERS CORNERED

Photographer: DOD MILLER
Printer: MIKE SPRY AT DOWNTOWN DARKROOM
Client: OBSERVER LIFE MAGAZINE
Title: SMOKERS CORNERED

Photographer: ANDY GREEN
Client: VAUXHALL
Commissioned by: LOWE HOWARD SPINK
Art Director: CHARLES INGE
System Operator: DAN TIERNEY

Photographer: ANDY GREEN
Client: VAUXHALL
Commissioned by: LOWE HOWARD SPINK
Art Director: CHARLES INGE
System Operator: DAN TIERNEY

Photographer: TESSA TRAEGER
Printer: TONY WHITE
Client: FINANCIAL TIMES
Commissioned by: JANE MULVAGH
Art Director: PATRICK KINMONTH
Make-up: JOHN GUSTAFSON AT PRESCRIPTIVES
Hair: MICHAEL AT MICHAELJOHN
Title: CHINESE COURTESAN'S JEWELLERY
SILVER, JADE & KINGFISHER FEATHERS

Photographer: TESSA TRAEGER
Printer: TONY WHITE
Client: FINANCIAL TIMES
Commissioned by: JANE MULVAGH
Art Director: PATRICK KINMONTH
Make-up: JOHN GUSTAFSON AT PRESCRIPTIVES
Hair: MICHAEL AT MICHAELJOHN
Title: CHINESE COURTESAN'S JEWELLERY
SILVER, JADE & KINGFISHER FEATHERS

Once again, we at Kodak Professional & Printing Imaging are delighted to sponsor the Portfolio category in this, the Thirteenth Awards.

The Awards come at the end of a year in which we have been honoured to continue our sponsorship of the Association Student Awards, launch our 'Exposure' scheme along with the 'Shot Right Here' exhibition for up and coming photographers, and sponsor the Association member's edition of 'Beyond The Lens'.

At Kodak, we are proud to be part of such a creative element in this otherwise commercial world, and we applaud all the photographers in The Thirteenth Awards on their deserved success.

CHRIS TOMBS
Director & General Manager – Professional & Printing Imaging
Kodak Limited

sponsored by

Photographer: NADAV KANDER
Printer: NADAV KANDER
Awarded: **SILVER**

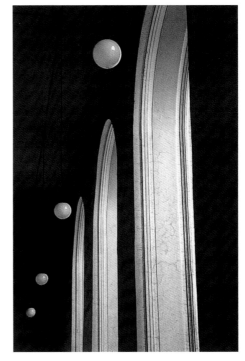

Photographer: NADAV KANDER
Printer: NADAV KANDER
Awarded: **SILVER**

Photographer: NADAV KANDER
Printer: BRIAN DOWLING (top)
Printer: DENNIS WATSON (bottom)
Client: MARLBORO
Commissioned by: BAINSFAIR SHARKEY TROTT
Art Directors: PAUL LEEVES & LEE GOULDING
Awarded: **SILVER**

166

Photographer: NADAV KANDER
Printer: BRIAN DOWLING
Client: MARLBORO (top)
Client: SILK CUT (bottom)
Commissioned by: BAINSFAIR SHARKEY TROTT (top)
Commissioned by: M & C SAATCHI (bottom)
Art Directors: PAUL LEEVES & LEE GOULDING (top)
Art Director: MARTHA REILLY (bottom)
Awarded: **SILVER**

Photographer: DAVID STEWART
Printer: SIMON BELL
Client: "CABBAGE"
Casting & Styling: SUE ODELL (bottom)
Costume: MANDY GOLDSMITH & WESLEY WEST (bottom)
Hair & Make-up: LAURA FRANKUM (bottom)
Model Maker: WESLEY WEST (top)

Photographer: DAVID STEWART
Printer: SIMON BELL (left)
Printer: 31 STUDIO/METRO (right)
Client: "CABBAGE" (left)
Client: CLARKS SHOES (right)
Commissioned by: McCANN ERICKSON (MANCHESTER) (right)
Art Director: DAVID PRICE (right)
Casting: SUE ODELL
Hair & Make-up: LAURA FRANKUM

Photographer: DAVID STEWART
Printer: SIMON BELL (left)
Printer: 31 STUDIO/METRO (right)
Client: TRADEPOINT (right)
Commissioned by: FAHRENHEIT (right)
Art Director: MARCUS HASLAM (right)
Casting: SUE ODELL (left)
Model Maker: WESLEY WEST (left)

Photographer: DAVID STEWART
Printer: SIMON BELL
Client: "CABBAGE"
Casting: SUE ODELL
Hair & Make-up: LAURA FRANKUM (top)
Model Maker: WESLEY WEST

171

Photographer: JEZ COULSON
Printer: MIKE SPRY AT DOWNTOWN DARKROOM
Client: THE OBSERVER
Commissioned by: INSIGHT PHOTOS
Title: RWANDAN REFUGEE CRISIS KIBUMBA
GOMA, RWANDA, ZAIRE BORDER AUGUST '94

Photographer: JEZ COULSON
Printer: MIKE SPRY AT DOWNTOWN DARKROOM
Client: THE OBSERVER (left)
Client: NEWSWEEK (right)
Commissioned by: INSIGHT PHOTOS
Title: RWANDAN REFUGEE CRISIS KIBUMBA. GOMA, RWANDA, ZAIRE BORDER AUGUST '94 (left)
Title: SERBIAN FIGHTERS AT CHECKPOINT ON THE ROAD TO BOSANSKI BROD. SERB HELD BOSNIA, NOVEMBER '93 (right)

Photographer: JEZ COULSON
Printer: MIKE SPRY AT DOWNTOWN DARKROOM (top)
Printer: MIKE DAVIS AT METRO (bottom)
Client: NEWSWEEK (top)
Client: VISIBLE EDGE (bottom)
Commissioned by: INSIGHT PHOTOS
Title: ETHNIC CLEANSING, MUSLIM PRISONERS AT THE TROPOLJE
SERBIAN PRISON CAMP, SERB HELD BOSNIA, NOVEMBER '93 (top)
Title: NELSON MANDELA AT ELECTION RALLY NEAR LADYSMITH,
NATAL, SOUTH AFRICA, APRIL '94 (bottom)

Photographer: JEZ COULSON
Printer: MIKE DAVIS AT METRO
Commissioned by: INSIGHT PHOTOS
Client: VISIBLE EDGE (top)
Client: NIGHT & DAY – MAIL ON SUNDAY (bottom)
Title: AWB (AFRIKANER RESISTANCE MOVEMENT) RALLY NEAR
RUSTENBURG DURING ELECTIONS, SOUTH AFRICA, APRIL '94 (top)
Title: CROATIAN SOLDIER AT THE DEATH OF A FRIEND,
MOSTAR, CROATIA, OCTOBER '93 (bottom)

175

For the second year running the Telegraph Colour Library is proud to sponsor The Association Awards.

Our continuing support of The Awards is in recognition of the important part they play within the industry, promoting excellence and providing recognition for creative endeavour. The Awards ultimately benefit all of us who share these goals and feel passionate about the quality of photography here in the UK.

We applaud all those who entered this year and congratulate the winners on their success.

TIM LUND

Director of Photography – Telegraph Colour Library

sponsored by

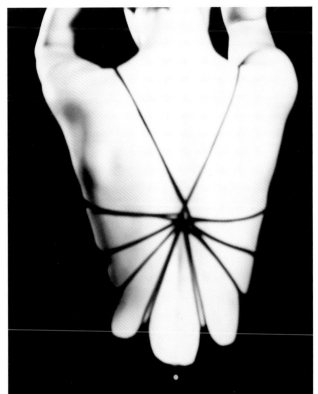 

Photographer: NADAV KANDER (left)
Selected by: ROSIE ARNOLD

Photographer: NADAV KANDER (right)
Selected by: MALCOLM VENVILLE

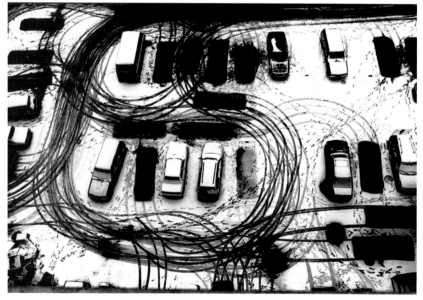

Photographer: NEIL HOLDEN (top)
Selected by: GILL DAVIES

Photographer: DERRICK SANTINI (bottom)
Selected by: CAROLINE METCALFE

Photographer: ANDREAS HEUMANN (top)
Selected by: PAUL BIDDLE

Photographer: ASHTON KEIDITSCH (bottom)
Selected by: CHARLES SETTRINGTON

179

Photographer: TIM O'SULLIVAN (top)
Selected by: KIKI KENDRICK

Photographer: GRAEME COOPER (bottom)
Selected by: PETER ROBINSON

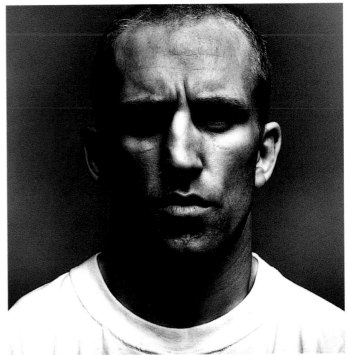

Photographer: DUNCAN McNICOL (left)
Selected by: DAVE BUONAGUIDI

Photographer: ANDREW SHAYLOR (right)
Selected by: PAUL WEBSTER

Photographer: ANTONIA DEUTSCH (left)
Selected by: GEOFF SMITH

Photographer: OWEN EDELSTEN (right)
Selected by: CHRIS CHEETHAM

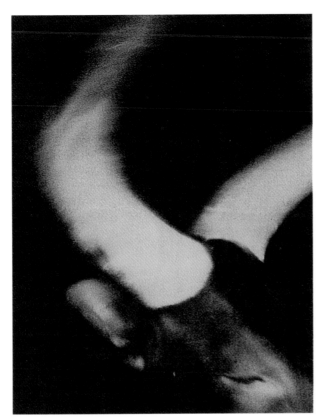

Photographer: MARC GOUBY (left)
Selected by: GARY HOLT

Photographer: GRANT DELIN (right)
Selected by: PETER MARLOW

The Association of Photographers is a non-profit making association which was first launched in 1968 as The Association of Fashion, Advertising and Editorial Photographers. Our principal aims have remained the same – to promote the highest standards of work and practice throughout the industry, and to protect and improve the rights of all professional photographers in the UK. We have our own Association Gallery and annual Awards, which are presented here and showcase our members' work. Our publications include Image magazine, Beyond The Lens, the Assistants' Awards and SUN catalogues, our Membership Services Directory, Standards of Practice package, Model Release Forms, Agent/Photographer Agreement Forms and a brand new Membership Handbook. As members of the BPLC, BCC and Pyramide Europe we work closely with other UK and European associations. We play a crucial role in improving standards of practice and were instrumental in negotiating changes which resulted in the Copyright, Designs and Patents Act (1988). We have a commitment to training and education and provide practical help and guidance to professional photographers.

For further information please contact:
The Association of Photographers
9-10 Domingo Street, London EC1Y OTA
Telephone 0171-608 1441.

FULL MEMBERS
Michael A'Court
Aart Aan de Weil
James Abelson
Geoff Adams
William Adams-Lingwood
Lorenzo Agius
Deyana Ahmadi
Tim Ainsworth
Stak Aivaliotis
Ricardo Alcaide
John Alflatt
Daniel Allan
Mel Allen
Christopher Ambrose
Simon Annand
Richard Ansett
David Anthony
Matthew Antrobus
John Aparicio
Peter Aprahamian
Miguel Arana
Caroline Arber
Jim Arnould
Sven Arnstein
Chris Arthur
Liz Artindale
Sue Atkinson
Kevin Attfield
Bryce Attwell
Mark Azavedo

Chris Bailey
Dequincey Bailey
Richard Bailey
Julian Bajzert
Susan Baker
Tom Baker
Jan Baldwin
Ron Bambridge
Bryan Bane
Jack Bankhead
Michael Banks
Zafer Baran
Edward Barber
Robert Barber
Christopher Barker
Colin Barker
John Barlow
Matthew Barlow
Martin Barraud
Peter Barry
Neil Barstow
Andy Barter
Greg Bartley
Karl Bartley

Ian Batchelor
Jennifer Bates
Simon Battensby
Peter Beavis
Martin Beckett
Terry Beddis
Jean-Luc Benard
Steve Benbow
Oliver Oliver
Geoffrey Benson
Adri Berger
Bert Berghuis
Theo Bergstrom
Derek Berwin
Paul Bevitt
Paul Biddle
Michael Bielby
Steve Bielschowsky
Berry Bingel
Peter Birch
Malcolm Birkett
John Bishop
Jacqui Bishop-Wornell
Martin Black
Michael Black
Anthony Blake
Patrick Blake
Chris Bland
John Blomfield
Christopher Booth
Tim Booth
Mike Botha
Roy Botterell
Clive Boursnell
Tony Bowran
Padraig Boyle
Adrian Bradbury
Richard Bradbury
Larry Bray
Geoff Brightling
John Brightmore
Tim Brightmore
Rob Brimson
Robin Broadbent
Michael Brockway
Alan Brooking
Paul Brooking
Martyn Brooks
Bruce Brown
Gareth Brown
Heather Brown
John Brown
Nick Brown
Simon Brown
Howard Brundrett
Gary Bryan

Alex Buckingham
Barry Bullough
Gerrit Buntrock
David Burch
Hugh Burden
Marc Burden
Desmond Burdon
Roger Burge
Adrian Burke
Alexandra Burke
Dan Burn-Forti
Paul Bussell

Anthony Cake
Julian Calder
Michael Caldwell
Julian Calverley
Andrew Cameron
Tommy Candler
Nick Carman
Clare Carnegie
Rory Carnegie
Wendy Carrig
Paul Carroll
David Cartledge
Ian Cartwright
Derek Cattani
Steve Cavalier
Phil Cawley
Barry Cawston
Jean Cazals
Sandra Cecil
Martin Chaffer
David Chalmers
David Chambers
Chris Cheetham
Don Chesser
Jane Chilvers
Pete Chinn
Jan Chlebik
Stuart Chorley
Ken Christie
Andy Christodolo
Philip Chudy
John Claridge
Nicholas Clark
Richard Clark
Michael Clement
Niall Clutton
Alwyn Coates
Patrick Cocklin
David Cockroft
Tessa Codrington
Stephen Coe
Stephanie Colasanti
John Cole

Andy Collison
Stephen Colover
Bryn Colton
Stuart Colwill
Adrian Cook
Tim Cook
Angela Coombes
Graeme Cooper
John Cooper
Ken Copsey
Suzy Corby
Rick Cordell
Tobi Corney
James Cotier
Gavin Cottrell
Jez Coulson
John Couzins
Christopher Cowan
Roger Cracknell
Bob Cramp
John Crane
Chris Craymer
Alun Crockford
Harriet Cullen
Lupe Cunha
Doug Currie
Kathy Curshen
Monica Curtin
William Curtis
Will Curwen
Colin Cuthbert

Lou D'Angelo
Nick Daly
Robert Daly
Jack Daniels
Geoffrey Dann
Alan Davey
Glyn Davies
Keith Davies
Nigel Davies
Duncan Davis
Mark Davison
Peter Dazeley
Julian de Havilland
Victor De Schwanberg
Patrice de Villiers
Mick Dean
Richard Dean
Peter Defty
Julian Deghy
Antonia Deutsch
James Diamond
Charles Dickins
Ken Dickinson
Julie Dixon

Michael Dmochowski
Stephen Dodd
Nick Dolding
Terence Donovan
Mark Douet
William Douglas
Philip Dowell
Robert Dowling
Chris Dreja
Tim Dry
Michael Duff
Paul Dunn
Michael Dunning
Dale Durfee
Craig Dyball
Michael Dyer

Julian Easten
Roger Eaton
Jillian Edelstein
Owen Edelsten
Ben Edwards
Andreas Einsiedel
Clint Eley
Mike Ellis
Robert Elsdale
Robert Enever
Andrew Errington
Dilwyn Evans
John Evans
Koren Evans
Laurie Evans
Frances Evelegh
Martin Evening

David Fairman
Douglas Falby
Simon Farnhell
Richard Faulks
Katherine Fawssett
John Fenton
Frank Fernandez
Nick Ferrand
John Ferrara
Des Fildes
Graham Finlayson
Conrad Fisher
Douglas Fisher
Julie Fisher
Claude Fisicaro
Tim Flach
Paul Flanagan
Adrian Flowers
Mark Follon
Colin Ford
Graham Ford

Max Forsythe
Wayne Forward
Paul Fosbury
Arthur Foster
Geoff Franklin
Don Fraser
Ian Fraser
Christopher Frazer-Smith
John Freebrey
Dean Freeman
Richard Freestone
Geoffrey Frosh
Clive Frost
Douglas Fry
Trevor Fulford
Bob Fyffe

Kate Gadsby
Ray Gaffney
Christopher Gale
Andy Gallacher
Michael Galletly
David Gamble
David Garcia
Steve Garforth
Glen Garner
Mark Gaskin
Mark Gatehouse
Paul Gates
Gerry Gavigan
Nick Georghiou
Tracey Gibbs
Tony Gilbert
David Gill
Andrew Glass
Richard Glover
Rolph Gobits
Tim Goffe
Tina Golden
Mike Goss
Marc Gouby
James Graham
Allan Grainger
Karl Grant
Tom Graty
Stephen Gray
Andy Green
David Greenwood
Kevin Griffin
Kenneth Griffiths
Susan Griggs
Kostas Grivas
Helen Groome
Guy Grundy
Lorentz Gullachsen
Andrew Gulland

Tim Gummer
David Guyon

Bill Halford
Andrew Hall
David Hall
Jon Hall
Maxine Hall
Stuart Hamilton
Keith Hammond
Alan Hampson
Christine Hanscomb
Michael Harding
Bob Harris
Gina Harris
Graeme Harris
Matt Harris
Tony Harris
Christopher Harrison
Mark Harrison
Simon Harsent
Philip Harvey
Mark Harwood
Laurie Haskell
Martin Haswell
Olly Hatch
Jason Hawkes
Laurie Haynes
Nigel Haynes
Stephen Hayward
Tim Hazael
Elisabeth Henderson
Graham Henderson
Frank Herholdt
Herbert Herzl
John Heseltine
Tim Hetherington
Andreas Heumann
Amanda Heywood
John Higginson
Shaun Higson
Ferguson Hill
John Hill
Martin Hill
Tim Hill
Hans Hilterman
Jane Hilton
Peter Hince
Adam Hinton
Bay Hippisley
Graham Hitchcock
Andrew Hobbs
Neil Holden
Philip Holden
Anthony Holmes
Lisa Hooley

Martin Hooper
Ian Hooton
Tony Hopewell
Charles Hopkinson
Jeremy Hopley
Christopher Hopper
Ed Horwich
Steve Hoskins
Kelvin Hudson
Neil Hudson
Alistair Hughes
Jamie Hughes
Malcolm Hulme
Phil Hunt
Tim Hunt
Tif Hunter
Judith Hurst
Tony Hutchings

Janet Ibbotson
Tim Imrie
Rowan Isaac

Roel Jacobs
Brian Jaquest
Phil Jason
Lu Jeffery
Robert Jobling
Hugh Johnson
Keith Johnson
Allan Jones
Hywel Jones
Paul Jones
Syriol Jones
Michael Joseph
Branka Jukic
Mark Junak

Ian Kalinowski
David Kampfner
Nadav Kander
Judith Katz
George Kavanagh
Michael Kay
Ashton Keiditsch
David Kelly
Howard Kemp
Jhon Kevern
Gavin Kingcome
Andrew Kingsbury
Howard Kingsnorth
Kevin Kingston
Ken Kirkwood
Peter Knab
Andy Knight
John Knill

Karen Knorr
Jonathan Knowles
Tim Knox
Henrik Thorup Knudsen
Tony Knuff
Bob Komar
Jess Koppel

Markku Lahdesmaki
Alastair Laidlaw
Peter Lake
Bob Lambert
Geoff Langan
Mark Lanning
Simon Larbalestier
Barry Lategan
Tony Latham
Heinz Lautenbacher
Peter Lavery
Mark Lawrence
John Lawrence Jones
Mike Laye
Simon Lee
Stephen Lee
Martin Leeks
Leon
Brian Leonard
Eleni Leoussi
Jerome LeRoy-Lewis
Chris Lewis
Simon Lewis
Patrick Lichfield
Jon Lippett
Martin Lipscombe
Peter Littlewood
Mark Livemore
George Logan
Derek Lomas
John Londei
Pauline Lord
Sandra Lousada
Jonathan Lovekin
Cornel Lucas
Grantly Lynch
Marcus Lyon
Carl Lyttle

John Mac
Neil MacKenzie
Matthews
Bruce Mackie
Niall Macleod
Tim MacPherson
Duncan MacQueen
Charlie Magee
Tom Main

Tim Malyon
Eric Mandel
Stephen Markeson
Barry Marsden
Alan Marsh
Anthony Marsland
John Mason
Ray Massey
Kiran Master
Robert Masters
Kit Constable Maxwell
Marcia May
Matthew May
Tony May
Linda McCartney
Fi McGhee
Michael McGoran
Christian McGowan
Iain McKell
Ian McKinnell
Kirsty McLaren
James McMillan
Duncan McNicol
Allan McPhail
Richard Meats
Barry Meekums
Nick Meers
Paul Mellor
Neill Menneer
James Merrell
James Meyer
Axel Michel
Mark Middlebrook
John Midgley
Peter Millard
Bob Miller
Diana Miller
Dod Miller
Glenn Millington
Allan Mills
Colin Mills
Paul Mitchell
Moggy
Caroline Molloy
Colin Molyneux
Graeme Montgomery
David Moore
Vernon Morgan
Adamo Morgese
Stephen Morley
Martin Morrell
Annie Morris
Greg Morris
Sara Morris
Trish Morrissey
Ralph Mortimer

Bill Morton
John Moss
Tim Motion
Sam Moxon
Chris Moyse
Lewis Mulatero
Tom Mulvee
James Murphy
Paul Murphy
Kelvin Murray
Allan Mushen
Peter Myers
Jay Myrdal

Horst Neumann
Alan Newnham
Patrick Nicholas
George Nicholls
Sanders Nicolson
Julian Nieman
Simon Norfolk
Gary-John Norman
Sally-Ann Norman
Taly Noy

Ian O'Leary
Tim O'Sullivan
Mike O'Toole
Jonathan Oakes
John Offenbach
Jerry Oke
Fleur Olby
Anthony Oliver
David Oliver
Andrew Olney
Steve Orino
Lizzie Orme
Gill Orsman
Tony Othen
Aernout Overbeeke
Chris Overton
Mike Owen
Gary Owens

Tony Page
Simon Page-Ritchie
Daniel Pangbourne
David Parfitt
Van Pariser
Clare Park
John Parker
David Parmiter
Nigel Parry
Mike Parsons
David Partner
Malcolm Pasley

David Paterson
Paolo Patrizi
Colin Peacock
Glen Percival
Glen Perotte
Kevin Peschke
Sergio Petrelli
Nick Philbedge
Nigel Phillips
Stephen Piotrowski
Tim Platt
Robert Pogson
Thomas Pollock
Mark Polyblank
Colin Poole
Russell Porcas
Sandy Porter
Fiona Pragoff
Richard Prescott
David Preutz
Nick Price
Susanna Price
Colin Prior
Ed Pritchard
Richard Pullar
Joshua Pulman
Justin Pumfrey
Con Putbrace

John Quinn

Ashton Radcliffe
Na'im Rahman
Ritva Raitsalo
Rodney Rascona
Peter Rauter
John Rawlings
Mark Rayner
Nick Read
Stuart Redler
Rocco Redondo
Darran Rees
Paul Rees
Steve Rees
Antonia Reeve
Mike Reeves
Jeremy Rendell
Ben Rice
Jim Rice
Ted Rice
Derek Richards
Trevor Richards
Eric Richmond
Tim Ridley
Martin Riedl
Nicholas Rigg

Andrew Roberts
Nick Roberts
Malcolm Robertson
Jeff Robins
Neil Robinson
Peter Robinson
Peter Rodger
Jonathan Root
Sarah Root
Taffi Rosen
John Ross
John A Ross
Joe Roughan
Dominic Rouse
Clive Rowat
Deborah Rowe
Kevin Rowley
David Rudkin
Stephanie Rushton
David Russell
Erik Russell
Mike Russell
Chris Ryan
Seamus Ryan

Houman Sadr
Russell Sadur
Gary Salter
Derrick Santini
Derek Scarbrough
David Scheinmann
Fran Schiller
Herb Schmitz
Derek Seagrim
Derek Seaward
Peter Seaward
David Seed
Claus Semmler
Geoff Senior
Charles Settrington
Mel Sewell
Andy Seymour
Carol Sharp
John Shaw
Andrew Shaylor
Mike St Maur Sheil
Jason Shenai
Peter Sherrard
Rod Shone
Steve Shooter
David Short
Richard Sibley
Paul Silverberg
Duncan Sim
Paul Simcock
Tim Simmons

Chris Simpson
Nick Simpson
John Sims
Tony Slade
Michael Smallcombe
Duncan Smith
Geoff Smith
Grant Smith
Mike Smith
Peter J Smith
Peter Smith
Robin Smith
Simon Smith
Andrew Snaith
George Solomonides
Simon Somerville
John Spragg
Brian Spranklen
Ian Spratt
Gino Sprio
Jeff Starley
Philip Starling
Dean Steadman
Charlie Stebbings
Moritz Steiger
Lars Stenman
Mark Stenning
Dan Stevens
Garry Stevenson
David Stewart
James Stewart
Jon Stewart
Simon Stock
Dennis Stone
Peter Story
James Strachan
Anthony Straeger
Caroline Summers
Kevin Summers
Richard Surman
Michael Swallow
David Swan
Mike Swartz
Andrew Sydenham
Edward Sykes
Lucinda Symons

David Tack
Cymon Taylor
Nigel Taylor
Sara Taylor
Calvey Taylor-Haw
Steve Teague
Luca Invernizzi Tettoni
Bert Teunissen
Han Chew Tham

Andrew Thomas
Colin Thomas
Martin Thompson
Peter Thompson
Steve Thompson
Peter Thorpe
Mark Tillie
John Timbers
David Tolley
Paul Torcello
Frances Tout
Jason Tozer
Tessa Traeger
Jonathan Trapman
Debi Treloar
Terry Trott
Pia Tryde Sandeman
Nick Turley
Adrian Turner
Corinne Turner
John Turner
Robert Turner
Leslie Turtle

David Usill

Mike Valente
Martin Vallis
Ariel Van Straten
Rohan Van Twest
Olaf Veltman
Mike Venables
Malcolm Venville
Stephen Vernon-Clarke
Manfred Vogelsanger

Richard Waite
Paul Wakefield
Sacha Waldman
Robert Walker
Andrew Wallis
John Walmsley
David Walter
Matthew Ward
Anthony Waring
Carl Warner
Malkolm Warrington
Ray Watkins
Denis Waugh
Uli Weber
Paul Webster
James Wedge
Matthew Weinreb
Rosemary Weller
Kenneth Wells
Peter Welton-Cook

Paul Wenham-Clarke
Christian Wenhammar
Philip West
Graham Westmoreland
Andy Whale
Simon Wheeler
Tim White
Will White
Terry Whiteman
Andrew Whittuck
Zanna Wilford
Reg Wilkins
Dai Williams
Glyn Williams
Michael Williams
Moy Williams
Peter Williams
Richard Williams
Barry Willis
Justin Windle
Chris Windsor
Paul Windsor
Tim Windsor
Martin Wonnacott
Peter Wood
Simon Wood
Stuart Wood
Tim Woodcock
Geoff Woods
Hilary Woolf
Adam Woolfitt
Ian Woollams
Jimmy Wormser
Andrew Wornell
Michael Wray
Tim Wren
George Wright
James Bissett Wright
Adrian Wroth
Jon Wyand

Graham Young
Mark Young

Za-Hazzanani
Jacek Jan Zaluski
Elizabeth Zeschin

ASSISTANT MEMBERS
Lindsy Agana
Ian Aitken
Mark Alcock
Jane Alexander
Nick Allen
Jonathan Andrew
Andy Andrews
Xenophon Ankrah
Richard Apperly
Jose Aragon
Robert Ashton

James Barlow
Nicholas Barnard
Adam Barnes
Samuel Barton
Loz Baylis
Dean Belcher
James Bell
Steve Benbow
Phillip Berryman
Charles Birchmore
Paul Blackshaw
Paul Blinston
Ian Boddy
Paul Born
Mike Boyle
James Braund
Martin Breschinski
Adrian Brown
Richard Brown
James Bunch
Simon Burch
David Burgess
Gavin Burke
Lesley Burke
Adrian Burt

Stuart Cain
Steve Callaghan
Andrew Catterall
Tamra Cave
Charlotte Challen
Ian Chamberlain
Nigel Charman
Oswald Cheung
Deepak Chohan
Jim Colley
Raffaele Colucci
Richard Cornwall
Pamela Cowan
Joann Crowther
John Cumming

Stephen Dagger

Nick David
Neil Davis
Adam Dawe
Mark Dawson
Gemma Day
Peter Day
William De La Hey
Al Deane
Grant Delin
Suki Dhanda
Kristina Dogge
Michael Donne
Christine Donnier-Valentin
Graeme Duddridge
Claudia Dulak
Russell Duncan
Gavin Durrant

Andy Eaves
Frea Eden
Raymond Ellis

Michael Fair
John Falzon
Guy Farrow
Gill Faulkner
Charlie Fawell
Michael Feather
Robin Feild
Indira Flack
Luke Foreman
Marty Forsyth
Eugenio Franchi
Julia Fullerton-Batten

Trish Gant
Matthew Gardner
Caroline Garside
Paul Gill
Victoria Gomez
Christopher Gonta
Michael Gough
Ally Graham
Juliet Greene
Andrew Greig

Stuart Hall
Carol Hallows
Jeremy Hardie
Nigel Harniman
Nicholas Harper
Michael Harvey
Sarah Harvey
Karen Hatch
Tim Hawkings
Lizzy Hearne

Luke Hickman
Jeremy Hilder
Anthony Hill
Jason Hindley
Logan Holmes
Robert Holmes
Jocelyn Horsfall
Colin Hoskins
Philip Howling
Graham Hughes
Ted Humble-Smith

Neal Jackson
Alan James
Nigel James
Annie Johnston
Michael Jones
Nick Judd

Christos Kalochoridis
Eddie Kay
John Kelly
Liam Kennedy
Glenn Kenworthy
Andrew Kruczek
Dana Kurlansky
Simon Kynaston
Tas Kyprianou

Sandra Lambell
Steffen Landua
Duncan Lawson
Neil Lawson
Dennis Lee
Shaky Lee
Simon Lefevre
Peer Lindgreen
Timothy Lofthouse
Tony Lumb
Paul Lund
Kerry Lyall

Stuart MacGregor
Jeremy Maher
Theresa Maloney
Helen Marsden
James Marsden
Suzanne Marshall
Patricia McGahan
Calum McIntosh
Colin McKay
Paul McNicholas
Simon Mills
Mash Mirza
Andy Morris
Gareth Munden

Antonio Munoz
Deborah Murray
James Murray

Richard Neall
Mark Newbold
Stephen Nicholls
Ian Nolan

Louise Openshaw
Edward Orange

Chris Parker
Louisa Parry
Susan Passmore
Craig Paulson
Jonathan Pegler
Bridget Peirson
Andrew Pendlebury
Martin Peters
Marcus Pietrek
Graham Piggott
Philip Pinchin
Lara Platman
Kate Plumb
Toby Pond
Sarah-Vivien Prescott
Sloane Pringle
Lucinda Pryor
Mark Purdom

Sarah Ramsay
Peter Reeves
Colin Renwick
Giles Revell
Marcel Reyes-Cortez
Roger Richards
Stephen Rodgers
Cesar Rodriguez-Duran
Stephen Rosewell
Darrell Russell

Debbie Sandersley
Paul Savage
Justin Scobie
Rex Scroggie
Dennis Seed
Andrew Shennan
Doug Sherring
Joao Silva
Gianluigi Siragusa
Simon Songhurst
Andrew Southon
Leon Steele
Allan Stone
Ashley Straw

Adrian Swift

George Tappeiner
Mark Tasker
Gary Taylor
Stephen Thomas
Alan Thornton
Peter Tizzard
Mark Turnbull

Rob Van Der Vet
Ras Verdi

Cameron Watt
Everton Waugh
Mathew Webb
Robert White
Joss Whittaker
Dave Willis
Andy Wilson
Tony Wong
Ben Wood
Mark Wood
Matthew Wright

James Yalden
Ian Yates
Steve Yeates

Paul Zak
Paul Zammit

SUPPORTIVE MEMBERS
Sue Allatt
Peter Bailey
Richard Baynes
Neil Burgess
Sally Byron-Johnson
Mark Cumming
David Gardiner
Ziggy Golding
Madeleine Hamel
Michael Hoppen
Niall Horton-Stephens
Jonathan Mallory
Jonathan Marsland
Pim Milo
Missy
Sally Neal
Charles Saddington
Tony Skinner
Tony Stone
Robert Toay
Germaine Walker
Laura Watts
Chantal Webber
Rebecca Wells

FRIENDS
Bernard Browne
Darren Hedges
Bel January
Bill Richmond
Kevin Roseblade
Keith Roughton
Jonathan Topps
Adam Tysoe
Nick Walton

AFFILIATED COMPANIES
Ceta Ltd
Fuji Photo Film Co.(UK) Ltd London
Hasselblad UK Ltd
Joe's Basement
Keith Johnson + Pelling Ltd
Kodak Professional & Printing Imaging
Nikon UK Ltd
Olympus Optical Co (UK) Ltd
Polaroid (U.K.) Ltd
Sky Photographic Services Ltd.
Williamson Carson & Co. Ltd.

AFFILIATED COLLEGES
Barking College
Berkshire College of Art & Design
Blackpool & the Fylde College
Bournemouth & Poole College of Art & Design
Carmarthenshire College of Technology & Art
Cheltenham & Gloucester College of Higher Education
City of Westminster College
Cleveland College of Art & Design
Dewsbury College
Falmouth College of Arts
Glasgow College Of Building & Printing
Glasgow School of Art
Kent Institute of Art & Design
Kingston University
Napier University
Newcastle College
Norfolk College of Arts & Technology
Norwich School of Art & Design
Plymouth College of Art & Design
Salisbury College
South East Essex College of Arts & Technology
Southampton Institute of Higher Education
Staffordshire University

THE SAWARD ROBERTS STUDIO

WISHES

THE ASSOCIATION OF PHOTOGRAPHERS

EVERY SUCCESS WITH

THE THIRTEENTH AWARDS

SAWARD ROBERTS

NORTHBURGH HOUSE
10 NORTHBURGH STREET
LONDON ECIV 0AY
TELEPHONE 0171 336 7480/81
FACSIMILE 0171 336 7481

**It's the most highly sophisticated piece
of machinery on the circuit.**

And here's a picture of a car.

There are few pieces of machinery that stand a chance of catching Damon Hill. Schumacher's Benetton may be one.

The Olympus OM3Ti in the hands of top sports photographer Jon Nicholson is the other. Indeed, Jon has spent the past two years on a mission to catch Damon in action. So why did he choose the OM3Ti for the job? For starters, lugging heavy equipment around circuits is no fun.

So the OM3Ti's hand-built body is made from titanium, which makes it lightweight and tough, yet durable for all weather conditions.

Once you're in position, the OM3Ti gives total creative control over your shot because it's fully manual. Even if your subject is Mr Hill gunning along at 200mph.

Forget about flat tyres, what about the dreaded flat battery? Not something you want to think about at the side of the track. And not something you'll ever have to. The OM3Ti houses a fully mechanical shutter. And also beneath its hand-built shell you'll find an ingenious feature called multi-spot metering.

Basically this takes selective readings of the same shot. Then a meter reads the light to provide you with highlight and shadow control.

But enough technical jargon. The best way to see what the OM3Ti can do is to see Jon Nicholson's photos for yourself. Last year he and Damon Hill produced the best selling book, "Damon Hill: A Grand Prix Year." And this year, Jon is putting together another called "Pole Position: The Inside Story of Williams-Renault."

A flick through either will show you the best machine on the circuit. As well as a few pictures of Damon Hill's Renault.

OLYMPUS OM3Ti

MODEL SOLUTIONS
AWARD WINNING MODELMAKERS

THE LEE FILTER SYSTEM UNDERGOING FIELD TRIALS

THE LEE FILTER SYSTEM UNDERGOING SEA TRIALS

THE LEE FILTER SYSTEM UNDERGOING HILL TRIALS

PHOTOGRAPHY BY DAVID NOTON, SHERBORNE, DORSET 01963 250498

LEE Filters

The Lee Filter System

PROVEN WORLDWIDE

Lee Filters, Central Way, Walworth Industrial Estate, Andover, Hampshire, SP10 5AN
Telephone : 01264 366245 Fax : 01264 355058

on the edge | frank herholdt

"I always feel **annoyed** by the smug, 'tasteful' work that the **average** landscape camera produces. There are **no tricks** in this picture, it's all in the **composition**, the **camera** and the **film**, EPP 120. Inspired by Balthus, a painter whose imagery always seems to me to have a **strange sexuality**, it's a **reaction** against 'good taste' and everything it stands for."

Kodak professional film | not what you expect

EPP 120 is the identification number of Kodak Ektachrome 100 Plus professional film. Kodak and Ektachrome are trade marks.

Image manipulation
and retouching on
Quantel Printbox.

Hand retouching and
Duplicate Transparencies.

UNICHROME

Unichrome Ltd.

8 - 10 Dryden Street, Covent Garden,
London WC2E 9NA

Tel: 0171 379 4755 / Fax: 0171 497 9542